As a newly married woman of one year in to what is now a blended family, I am honored to have had the opportunity to read this book. I am dealing with the challenge of creating a family with five adult sons (three of whom are his and two mine) and one not yet accepting of his father's choice to marry. But God! I pray your book will be a blessing to many as God continues to use you to share the lessons you have learned to help make blended families work. Your advice from Rev. Porter, the beloved man that he still is, shall continue to be with me as well: There is no such thing as step-love!" And to this and your book, I say, "Amen! Let blended families continue to blend in Love!" –

Rev. Dr. Janae Moore, Founder and CEO
Taranga House Spiritual Retreat & Practice Center
Adjunct Professor and Author of *What is That Thing,*
Poetry for Spiritual Introspection & Dialogue that leads to Action

Yours, Mine, and Ours

Yours, Mine, and Ours

A Mother's Guide to Blending a Family (but Anybody Can Use It)

Dana A. Porter Ashton, MACC, MDiv.

To order additional copies of this book, contact:
Xlibris
1-888-795-4274
www.Xlibris.com
Orders@Xlibris.com
777739

ACKNOWLEDGEMENTS

This is always the difficult part because I don't want to leave anybody out. So, I'll do it this way:

God, I THANK YOU for my entire family and friends, namely, Maurice (143), Brittany, Marcellus, Malcolm, and Monay. Robin, Eugene, Deborah, Jackie (RIP), and Melvin.

To my parents, who epitomized family and taught me how to love unconditionally.

To my father, the late Rev. Dr. William Robert Porter, who never got the chance to write his story, but I pray is proud of me for writing mine.

To my mother, Mrs. Doris A. Porter, the one who showed me how to mother and mothers not only the four of us (my sisters and I), but thousands of others who consider themselves her sons and daughters.

To Mike Jones who planted the idea that my journey to mothering was important. Dr. Valdes Snipes-Bennett and team for the direction you gave and the work you put in to completing this project.

To you, the reader, for picking this book up and reading it.

PREFACE

I believe I first heard the term *blended family* when I watched the movie, *Yours, Mine, and Ours* with Lucille Ball and Henry Fonda. I know what you're thinking, "that wasn't Lucille Ball and Henry Fonda, that was Rene Russo and Dennis Quaid." And you are correct; however, the original one came out in 1968 (watch it if you ever get a chance) and that was my first time hearing the term used. Back then, it was a rarity, or maybe nobody talked about it. I'm not sure, but either way, the movie industry considered the topic "risqué". Down through the years, the topic has become so normal that there's an actual definition of blended family listed in Webster's Dictionary. (see definition section)

There are so many books and self-help guides on blended families; therefore, I'm grateful you picked this one up to read. Now, I'll be honest with you from the very beginning and tell you this one is a little different. By different, I mean when I was writing the book I wrote it as though you and I were sitting at the table talking openly and candidly about this thing called a blended family. You'll hear my experience, my heart, my wit, and my actual experiences. Trust me, I'm not trying to portray myself as anything except a wife who learned the hard way on how to blend a family.

As you read this book, I'm hoping you'll feel as though you and I are sitting at the table chatting about a blended family. Although I'm a mother writing from my point of view, it doesn't matter if you're a father, grandmother, cousin, or godparent – blending a family can be a challenge.

I realize that I'm not the only one in this situation—as the blended family is becoming more and more popular. The chances of you finding yourself in a blended family circumstance are very possible, and I wanted to share what I did to make mine work. It's not long—just a few guiding thoughts on what worked for me that I want to share with you. All of them may not be your story or your situation, so take what you can use, tweak them to fit your particular situation, and know you are not alone.

Peace.
Dana

INTRODUCTION

First let me introduce myself. My name is Dana Aurore Porter Ashton. I am a woman, a wife, a mother, a preacher, an employee, a motivator, and now, an author. I've been married twice (still to #2) and inherited four children who call me "Ma" and "Ma Dana." I have a Bachelor of Science degree in Human Development, a Master of Arts degree in Christian Counseling, and a Master of Divinity. In the midst of all that, I had the amazing task of blending a family—twice. Yet, with all of my accomplishments and all of my degrees, they couldn't help me with the task of taking all these people and setting up a home. Believe it or not, it was my desire to have a family that taught me what I needed to do to make my blended family work.

I am the youngest of four girls. Both of my parents were present in the home; and like most little girls, I dreamed of one day getting married and having children. It never crossed my mind that my adult life would look any different from my parents. I mean, after all, they were married for over 55 years when my father passed in 2008; so why wouldn't my life be the same? What a wake-up call I received when I looked up and my life was nothing like theirs. Oh, I'm not complaining. In fact, I'm grateful for my life's journey because it shaped me into the woman that I am. Enough of that....let me get on with it.

I was never able to birth children from my womb, but God loved me so much He blessed me with one girl (the oldest) from my first marriage and one girl and two boys from my second marriage. All of them are grown now, but they are still my babies. They came to me at different ages and stages in my life and in theirs. The oldest girl lived with her father and I from the age of four until the time we separated. After we separated, she remained with her father, but visited me on the weekends. When I remarried, one of the boys lived with his father and I while his brother and sister would visit on the weekends. During the summers, we (second husband and all four of the children) would take as many family trips as possible, but a lot of our time was spent just trying to get along.

I'll be honest...we've had ups and downs—but through it all, we made it. It wasn't perfect and there were times we had to stay out of each other's way so it wouldn't "get ugly." But one day, something happened. I looked up and we were a family—a great big loud loving Nation; and for that, I'm grateful.

And so, I dedicate this book to Brittany, Marcellus, Malcolm, and Monay, with all the mother love I have in me.

DEFINITION

Blended Family

"A family that includes children of a previous marriage of one spouse of both" (Merriam Webster)

"Also called a step family, reconstituted family, or a complex family, is a family unit where one or both parents have children from a previous relationship, but they have combined to form a new family. The parents may or may not then have children with each other." (LoveToKnow)

"A family consisting of a couple, the children they have together, and their children from previous relationships." (The Oxford Dictionary)

"A family consisting of a couple and their children from present and all previous relationships." (Online Dictionary)

"A family...." (Me)

Yours + Mine = Ours

AND SO IT BEGINS.....

Being labeled a blended family is not a negative but a positive. When I married my first husband and learned his daughter would be living with us, I had mixed emotions. I didn't know what to expect so I was nervous she would not like me, afraid I would mess up, excited because I was finally going to be a mother, and weepy because I didn't birth her. It wasn't long before all of my fears and concerns were put to rest and it wasn't long before I understood I needed to have a conversation with her. You see, she was 4 years old when she started living with us and had already established relationships with her mother's family. Now, here was this woman, who married her father, entering her life full force. Don't get me wrong, she loved me, but she was very aware that there was a change in her life. One day, as I was picking her up from the babysitter, her great aunt (the one who she lived with before us) was leaving. We met each other in the hallway and the look on her face was one of confusion. Just then, I heard the babysitter say, "You don't have to choose. It's okay to love them both". At that moment, you could almost see the stress lift from her face and she ran to hug me. The conversation I alluded to earlier was the one that was reiterated when the babysitter was with her. When we got in the car, I explained having two families gives her two times the love and two times the support and two times the Christmas presents.

After my second marriage, I found myself having the same conversation with the three who came. Although only one lived with their father and I, they were much older and truly had established lives.

They were close to their mother and didn't always want to come and visit. Thank the Lord I was able to recognize it and decided the next time they came over, I would tell them the same thing I told their older sister, "You don't have to choose". When my children learned they didn't have to choose between their mother and I, or spending time with one family over the other, they felt at ease with life.

What I didn't want to do was tell them it was me or her. Why? Listen, kids these days need all of the support, all of the love, all of the hope, and all of the joy they can get and having a blended family provides double support. Never let anyone define your family or look at you cross-eyed because they don't understand it. We don't wear labels… we just are.

What follows are steps we have taken to help make our blended family be what we are: a family.

In Our House: Establishing the rules of your house and having to explain the difference

One of the major discussions we had at the very beginning was our house rules. Actually, the discussion took place before the kids came. It was important we remained on the same page when it came to house rules—especially when the house rules changed from one house to the next. We were patient with the kids because there was a difference between the two homes, and we wanted them to have an opportunity to adjust. We found it important not to remain so stuck and so rigid that we were not willing to make adjustments regarding the house rules. When they started living with us, we threw some things out and we pulled some things in based on our needs. See, on paper, the rules looked great; however, in reality, some things needed tweaking. The interesting thing is after about a week or so, the kids adapted well and the rules became a way of life.

Make it work: Taking a "by any means necessary" approach to blending

My father, when faced with a difficult situation, used to say, "Make it work". When I found myself in the situation of trying to blend a family, I would encourage myself and declare I would take on the "make it work by any means necessary" approach. I knew I wanted our family to be a family and I resolved within myself to do what I needed to do to get us there. Don't get me wrong, each one of us had a role, but I was aware as the woman (the neck), I needed to do what I had to do to make our family work. If it meant hugging and loving up on the children, then that's what I did. If it meant listening to them fuss about having to spend the night with us, then I did that as well.

What I didn't do was take it personally. I consider myself to be a very caring and compassionate person and it was important for me to remain stable and not think this family was only about me. It was not. It was about pulling adults and children from different backgrounds, lifestyles, values, and morals together to create a loving family. Trust me, we had our difficult times but we also had our wonderful times. Let me give you an example of how I had to take a "by any means necessary" approach to blending the family.

One Good Friday, I was asked to preach one of the Seven Last Words of Jesus. The church was full and the Spirit was high. As I finished the sermon, I remember jumping up and when my feet hit the ground as I came back down, something happened in my knee that caused me so much pain, I thought I had broken something. My husband (#2) saw my face and motioned for me to sit down. When service was over, he and my daughter (the oldest one from #1) came over to me to check on me. I told them what happened and he went to pull the car up in front of the church. My daughter helped me walk out the door and since most of the people were still there, many were following us to make sure I made to the car. And then it happened! He gets out of the car to help me, she tells him she has me, he tells her he has me, and they begin to cuss each other out!!! Right there in front of the church!!! I was so embarrassed and angry I told both of them, in my quiet, teeth clinched, I'm disgusted with both of you (in my mother voice I said), "Get in the car right now. I can do it by myself". Once in the car, I said some things, much of which I'm ashamed to tell you, that needed to be said. What I can share with you is I acknowledged both of them were concerned about me and loved me. I also acknowledged that I appreciated what they were doing but because of this new family life, we had to learn how to get along. I told them they had to figure it out on their own because my brain would be focused on trying to figure out what was going on with my knee. When we got home, I made my way to my bed, took some medicine and went to sleep, leaving the two of them alone. When I awoke the next morning, I could hear noise downstairs in the kitchen. When I hobbled in, the two of them were making breakfast and talking as though nothing had happened the night before. Interestingly enough, we never talked about it again.

The lesson here is the "by any means necessary" approach means figuring out when you need to speak up or when you need to sit it out and let them figure it out.

Since I'm sharing, I'd like to offer this story as another example of taking the "by any means necessary" approach to blending the family.

One summer right after I remarried, I looked around the house and realized I had no pictures of "US". I had lots of pictures of my oldest daughter but none of the entire group. I then looked at the kids and how they were spread out and not interacting with each other. It hit me that I needed to fix that, so, I gathered up all four children, got my camera, and drove to the park. We had an impromptu mini photo session and what I saw amazed me. Whereas nobody was interested in playing together at home, the comradery soon began to reveal itself as I allowed the kids to choose the poses. It was refreshing to see them take over and even begin to play and tell me to capture them playing together and laughing. As soon as we finished, I stopped at the store to have the pictures developed quickly. When we got the pictures, the kids and I sat down and I let them choose the ones they wanted to hang on the wall. Once they decided, I had the pictures enlarged and framed and all of a sudden, our house started to look like our home. It became a place where all of the children could come and see themselves as part of the family.

The lesson of the "by any means necessary" approach here means as the parent, you may need to look at the big picture and walk in the shoes of the children. Although they never said anything, I'm sure it must have been uncomfortable for the kids to come to a house where they were told they were a part of a family and not see themselves. This approach served a dual purpose, to bring the children together for something fun and to let them feel like part of the family.

My family and me: What do you want your family to look like and what are you willing to endure to get it?

Early on I mentioned having the "make it work" attitude; and right here is where I want to ask you, "What do you want your family to look like?" I mean, what role does each person play? Do you want it to look like the family you were raised in or do you want it to look like the family of your best friend where it all looked nice? Here is where I caution you. Remember what you see is the product and not necessarily the process. So let me break it down even more. What product do you want and what is the process you plan to take? I wish I could give you the answer, but this is one you and Dad have to consider--preferably before the blend begins. I thought I had no reference point because my parents were married and together my entire life; but in reality, that was my reference point. I wanted my family to look like my family because I love my family. I wanted them to know that love and experience that love. I wanted them to be able to laugh and enjoy each other's company and at the same time be able to discuss anything. I wanted them to learn how to listen to all of the conversations taking place at one time, and to be able to interject in each one. I wanted them to learn the family grace and participate in my family's traditions. What do you want your family to look like—and what will you do to get it?

Step children...Daddy's advice: "No such thing as step love"

When I first became what I called, a step-mother, my father pulled me to the side and made it clear I should never refer to my daughter as a step child because there was no such thing as step love. I mentioned before I've never given birth to children; but I must say the ones God has sent me have my real love. Nope, no step-love here! My mantra soon became, "I didn't birth you from my belly but from my heart". I miss my Daddy.

No, you can't call me Mommy: So what will they call you?

When I first started out on this journey of blending, I knew my oldest daughter couldn't call me by my first name, so I gave her options. She initially said that she wanted to call me "Mommy", and I told her no because her mommy would be sad (she was 3 at the time). So, I researched and came up with two options: Aunt Dana (obvious reasons) or MaMa (Swahili for mother). She chose MaMa. When she went back and referred to me as such, she was told she didn't have to call me that and my name was Dana. Of course, that didn't sound right to her, so when she came back, she told me, and this is what I did: I told my mother. Yes, that's right; I told my mother because I knew she would give me wise counsel—and that she did. I called the other house and spoke with the mother figure. I asked her if she was called by her first name by the three year old child; and when she said, "Absolutely not"; I replied, "Neither am I." I explained how we came up with the name and what it meant. Then I explained I was not trying to take the place of her mother, but I was in fact, mothering her and would be respected as such. As the years passed, MaMa became "Mama" and soon became "Ma." When I married him (#2), for those three, I went from Ms. Dana to "Ma Dana"—a title I wouldn't trade for the world. Choose a name that you come up with, but no first names. It's a matter of respect.

I want you to understand that I'm not going anywhere; so, let's make it work: How to tell the other mother/family member that you're going to be involved

One of the most difficult things for any woman to realize is another woman will have a hand in raising her child. It doesn't matter what the role is, it's a fact. Something happens and we become very defensive and see this as a negative instead of a positive. For me, I not only had to share the fact that I wasn't going anywhere and I would be involved in the life of the children with one of the mothers, but I also had to share it with her family members. Once I said it, and not in a nasty or hateful manner, life was a little simpler and I no longer had to take a back seat, allowing just the father to make decisions in their upbringing.

There came a time, in both marriages, when I had to explain we were in this together and I was not the enemy. Before I share the events, let me clarify and say that in both cases, I believe I was questioned because of the evil stepmother stigma from fairytales. And in both cases, I had to explain I was not that person. Honestly, I don't really know what made me address it except for the fact that at the very moment it came up, something in me said that was the right time.

So, here are two examples from each marriage:

#1 The night before our oldest daughter was to come and live with us, we went to her aunt's house to pick up a few things so that her bedroom would be ready and feel like home. I was already tired from having worked all day, running home, putting final touches on her bedroom, quickly preparing and eating dinner, and then driving to their house, so when we got what we needed, I was ready to leave. As he and I were at the door, the aunt stopped me and said, "You better not do anything to her or hurt her". Well, this caught me by surprise because in all of our interactions with them and the child, I had never given her a reason to think I would harm the child, or at least I didn't think I had. When she said it, I looked directly in her face and what came out shocked not only my husband, but it also shocked me. What came out was, "Let me tell you something. First of all, if I was going to do anything to her, I would have done it already. Second, I don't know where this is coming from, but I am not the evil stepmother in fairytales. My family doesn't know anything about step-love. So, put your mind at ease and stop all this foolishness, she's coming to live with us". After I finished, I turned and walked out the door leaving everyone, including my husband, standing there with their mouth hanging open. When he came outside, he told me he was proud of the way I handled myself because he was getting ready to say something. I told him thank you and we went home. She came to live with us the very next day.

#2 The youngest son had been living with us for a little over a year. I was commuting to Baltimore for work and the price of gas was on the rise. My husband (#2) and I talked at length and decided the best thing to do was to move to Baltimore. We were coming home from church one Sunday and my cell phone rang. When I answered, on the other end was his mother telling me I had some nerve, taking her son to Baltimore without her permission. She went on to tell me she wasn't going to let him go and if we took him, it would be considered kidnapping. It was crazy! My husband looked at me and mouthed, "What's wrong?". I put my hand up to tell him to hold on and then I told her I would call her back because I was not going to have the conversation in front of the boy. When I hung up, I looked at my husband and said softly, "She's crazy". When I got home, I had some time to calm down and think and when I called her back, it was like night and day. She was pleasant enough and as I explained we were not kidnapping him, but trying to make some changes for our family and she had not been told because the idea was still new, she seemed better. I also explained we would work something out and he could visit her as often as he liked or as often as she wanted, and although we would not be driving him to her every weekend, she was free to come and pick him up. About 3 weeks later, we moved and it all worked out fine.

It's not easy, but it can be done: Trying to get everybody on the same path is difficult; however, it is possible

I would love to tell you that every day was butterflies and unicorns, but I'm not going to lie to you. Sometimes it was bumblebees and wild goats; but we made it. Here's the thing to remember: In reality, few things, when there's more than one person involved, happen overnight. Getting everybody on the same page felt like forever, but it was worth it. Those are the times you close your eyes, take a deep breath, and picture in your mind's eye everybody walking on the same path. Not necessarily holding hands and singing "Kum Bah Yah", but at least on the same road.

My greatest challenge came during our first Thanksgiving as a new family after the second marriage. Whew! All four of the children were there, husband was working, and I was left to try and prepare Thanksgiving dinner for 15 additional members of my family, including my parents. What a sight! I gave each child an assigned dish to cook and a specific time to cook it. Things were going well and then for some reason, the oldest one developed an attitude with me. I don't even remember the reason (not that teenagers need a reason), all I know is that it took all I had not to punch her lights out. Instead, I tried even harder to include her because I didn't know what else to do. I walked away often to gather myself and I finally told her it was time to get her attitude in check because this was her "new normal"; all of us together cooking in the kitchen and working together. She didn't really come around until about two days later (the day after Thanksgiving) and I'll admit I was glad when she left to go with her father on Thanksgiving Day (don't judge me 😊) because she was really bringing us down. Only kidding. I think she needed the time away to get herself together and to process the "new normal".

The purpose of this book is to help you not make the same errors I made and to inform you of some possibilities. This is the moment I'll encourage you to try and not get frustrated when you feel like you're the only one interested in becoming a family. Don't do like I did and pacify it, only frustrating myself. Instead, when you feel the frustration rise, try not to respond in frustration, it only exasperates the situation. Do what you must to give yourself time to deal with the feeling. Walk away, turn on music, cry (not in front of them), sing a song, call a friend, just don't lash out at them; after all, it's not their fault. Be patient and laugh out loud. Celebrate the new life everyone is reaching to attain, and just "roll with it" and before you know it, your journey will include the entire family and you'll look back and see that everyone is on the same path.

Holidays: Who goes where and for how long?

Holidays were always interesting because it varied each year. For us, we (or, at one point, the court) worked out the schedule ahead of time, and as the kids got older, we let them decide where they wanted to be. Now, I must admit that some holidays were (and still are) non-negotiable. For instance: Christmas Eve. The tradition in my family is that we all gather at my parent's house, read the Christ story, eat, sing, exchange gifts, and share memories; therefore, I wanted the kids to share in that experience. Since we eventually finished around 9:30-10:00 p.m., they were free to go wherever they like—and even spend Christmas Day with others. When they were in school, the longer breaks, like summer, winter, and spring breaks were shared—especially since most of the time neither parental unit took any time off from work to keep them occupied. That meant enrolling them in camp, finding child-care for them, or even calling on family members to help out. I think the main point I want to make here is holidays can be an emotional time, and it's important for the adults to communicate early, honestly, openly and remain flexible so the kids aren't caught in the middle.

We're in this together – A message for the village

At one point, I had to bring everybody together—my side, his side, our side—to talk. We needed to be clear that the blend happened smoothly without any outside force messing it up. It's easy for that one "crazy aunt" or that one "loud cousin" to say something about how many kids we have—albeit jokingly—and cause a rift in the family. My immediate family—just like his—was put on notice that our children were our children…they were a part of the Nation (what my sisters call our family). My parents were "grandma and grandad"—and my sisters were "aunt". If you're related to me, then you're related to them. Believe it or not, it was easy to do and they all loved it.

Stop trying to do this alone…Ask for help – use your support system and seek help when you need to

I know that right about now you're thinking, "Wow, this has really helped me. I can do this"—and that's great, but slow down. You can't do it alone. It's okay to ask for help. I know you know other women who are trying to blend a family…and did it. Ask them how. Ask them to give pointers. Ask your own family members to help you. Asking them to watch the kids for a couple of hours because you need a break doesn't mean you're a failure or you don't like the kids. Remember, this may be something very new for you. Maybe they didn't live with you at first or maybe you never saw them. And now they have invaded your space. Life is different now. Ask for help so you don't become bitter and mean and take it out on them. Always remember that the children didn't ask for any of this.

How much do I love you? So much so that I wish I had you myself: Letting the kids know you love them

I remember when I became "MaMa" to my first daughter. She was about 2 years old when I met her. Believe it or not, she wanted nothing to do with me. We – her father and I - would go for walks with her and sing songs. When I would sing, she would stop. That still makes me laugh today because we're as close as we are. When I shared that this little girl had a special place in my heart with a friend of mine (who was also the head of a blended family), she shared her experience with me in becoming another mother to her husband's children. She said she would ask them, "How much do I love you?" and the response was always, "So much so I wish I had you myself". That declaration moved me so much that when the time was right (no specific time, I just knew it was the right time), I taught my new daughter. Although she was young, she caught on very well. I've done that with each child since that time. The interesting thing is it took me longer to share it with the 2nd husbands' children than with the first. I think it's because they were so much older when I met them and established a relationship.

I recently asked the youngest girl if I actually taught her the question and answer. She said, "Yes", but that she didn't agree with it. This is what she wrote: "Sorry, that doesn't work. You did "have" me. You birthed a HUGE part of me that never would have developed if I hadn't first: Met you—and then was raised by you." Yep, sometimes you just never really know (and yes I cried when I read it 💻).

We're all on the same team so don't even try it: The best way to discourage the kids using one parent against the other

Kids will be kids. I did it and more than likely, you did it. Did what? We all tried to use one parent against the other. Not necessarily in a negative way, but in order to get what we wanted. That didn't work in our house because we kept constant communication flowing. As parents (yours, mine, and ours), we still had to parent our children and that meant talking to one another even when we didn't want to; because in reality, it wasn't about our feelings but about the well-being of the children. We know our children and we know when something doesn't sound right. So when my daughter would say something that didn't set right with me, I would get on the phone and call her dad and ask him about it to confirm and vice versa. When the kids know that the adults are working together and on the same team, they are less likely to use this approach.

I've already handled that: Getting the adults to trust one another when a situation has been handled – Communication is the key

When there is a possibility that there are at least four adults involved in decision-making, communication and trust are key. Depending on the situation, a decision may need to be made immediately; but if communication remains open, then whoever is making the decision should have an idea of the group's consensus. I think I can say simpler: Talk with each other enough so you trust the decision-maker. If a kid sees dissention in the ranks, they will feed on that and it becomes a source of manipulation for them. Avoid it by letting them see a united front (even if it's a warzone behind closed doors) when decisions regarding them are made. Then after you handle a situation, share it with the adults to further ensure everybody is on the same page. I know you might not like it, but it's not about the adults—it's about the kids.

Helping the kids find their place in everyone's life and feel like a part of the entire village

In our house (both times), family is family and children are loved unconditionally. All of our kids are included in my family (remember I didn't birth any of them) and treated as such. They receive gifts, are included in and expected to attend all events, and check in periodically with Grandma (my mother). Even as adults and "almost" adults, they know they are a part of the Porter Nation and have our prayers and support. Our closest friends are called "aunt" and "uncle"—and their children—cousins. Kids just really want to know they belong, are loved, and in the midst of all of the changes, they belong. Make sure your kids know they are loved and are a part of your extended family. Remember they're not step children, but children and they look to you for validation.

Dealing with the hard stuff....

Invasion of the other people: Life is different now-what happened to just us?

After my second marriage, it was just he and I. And then it happened. After about a year of marriage, we got the call. You know the call… "You need to come get him". Now here's the thing….he spent lots of time with us and it was not a problem; however, visiting is very different than living. Living means they never go home because they are home. I must be honest and say it was a transition period for me; because by this time, I had only the one girl and she lived with her dad. Also—I had no idea what to do with a boy. I quickly learned you do the same things, but without all of the hugging and kissing. I mean I loved on him and we spent time together, but there were times I wondered, "What happened to just us?" Again, it was an adjustment period, and I knew if it was going to work, I had to set boundaries. Those boundaries included setting certain "rules". Nothing crazy; but rules such as, "My bathroom is my bathroom. If the door to the room is closed, knock first; and don't leave the house without letting me know. When you come in, let me know." Simple rules or rather standards, which were expected, made the invasions easier. I must also say that the word "invasion" sounds so sci-fi and far out. In reality, having other people in the house after a long period of time was a little far out for me; but once I learned to embrace it, set up boundaries, and kept it moving, life wasn't so bad.

Do you love me? Loving them even when they don't want to be loved by you

I think I talked a little about this in one of the earlier tips; however, I wanted to elaborate a little more. Simply put—kids know when you're faking and they aren't always going to like you, care for you, or even listen to you, so you know they won't love you. Right here, I can hear my father's voice saying, "You aren't responsible for how others treat you, but you are responsible for how you treat others". You're the adult and consider this: you are the outsider. You're the one infiltrating the family and it's not always pretty; however, you are responsible/required to love in spite of it all. I didn't say kiss up… I said love them in spite of them. Never lower your standards or your character to the level of someone younger than you. It's not worth it and honestly, maybe your actions will speak volumes and teach the lesson of love.

So, who's really in charge here? Who's in charge when all the kids get together?

Our full house consisted of my husband and I and four young people. It was important that order be established if we were to function without killing each other. That meant we had to determine who was in charge. Now, when I say "in charge", I don't mean for babysitting purposes. For me, in charge meant all of the young people understood that hubby and I were a team, and we ruled our household. Not that they ever did it, but we had to be clear that the other parents had no say in what we do in our house (I'll address this more in #22). As the adults, we made the decisions together about everything from discipline to dinner. If only one of us was home, it didn't matter who you belonged to, you were part of the family. Let me break it down even more: If I wasn't home, mine knew he was in charge, and if he wasn't home, his knew I was in charge. Now here comes something important: COMMUNICATION IS KEY (wow another all caps statement🖥). It was imperative that he and I communicate with each other to know what was going on; therefore, we could support the other. That meant

I had to trust him and he had to trust me to have input in the lives of our children. Oh, it was hard at first for all of us because I was so used to making decisions on my own, as was he. But when the reality hit we would have four kids in the house for several weeks, we had to push that aside and work it out. Oh, and by the way, the kids never knew when we didn't agree. When we stood before them, we were a united front.

You're not my mother: Believe me, these words will come in some form--sooner or later

People kept telling me to expect it. They kept saying I'd hear the words eventually, but I refused to believe it. I mean after all—I had been there to dry tears, take her shopping, saying prayers and tucking her into bed. Yeah, well….it came—when I least expected it—right out of those lips I had just fed. We were leaving the mall, and I told her she couldn't have something; and for some reason, the conversation escalated. And just like that, I heard it. "I want my mother. You're not my mother". When I heard the words, I understood the emotional roller-coaster because I went from hurt to shock to anger to pissed to broken… back to angry, and finally landed on disbelief. I could not believe she would say those words to me. So this is what I did: I drove home, sent her to her room, went into my room (still fussing), called him upstairs, and told him what happened. I could still hear her in her room, so I took the phone in and told her to call her mother and tell her to come and get her—knowing that she didn't have a number. And then I told her (or maybe screamed), "And don't think you're taking anything we bought with you". I went back into my room and wept for her and for myself. Let me tell you why. I knew she loved me, but I also realized the past weekend was yet another broken promise from her mother; and what I was witnessing was the way an eight-year-old handled the hurt. I let her father go in and handle it, and then I went in and held her close to me. I didn't apologize and neither did she, but from that day forward, she never said it again. Sometimes we have to look beyond the "what" in order to figure out the "why".

I'm not trying to replace anybody...I'm the addition: Acknowledging your role in the family

I mentioned earlier it's difficult for a woman to come to the realization that another woman will be involved in raising her children. Well, it's also difficult for the children to understand that your role is not to replace their mother. The funny thing is, though I never said it, it was the mother of my second husband's children who presented the concept of being an addition to the family. It made so much sense to me I embraced it even more and began to speak it. Now listen to what I realized when I embraced it: I realized both of us as mothers have a different purpose and a different role in their lives! She is the firmer one—the one with the history—the one who knows their every move. In contrast, I am the one who talks about anything—the one who shares life lessons and stories; the one who will stop and pray in a hot minute; and the one who encourages them to take leaps of faith. See, there are two of us; but we offer different gifts and roles.

Dude, I'm on your side: When all the kids, including his, prefer you to him

Because the mother is usually the nurturer, sometimes, no, most of the time, the kids tend to gravitate to that nurturing nature— usually leaving dad kind of "out there" waiting for a hug. In my own experience, the kids come to me for the hugs, kisses, prayers, and motivational moments; but subsequently, they go to him when they need money or hard advice. If you're not careful, that in itself can cause yet another challenge and unnecessary arguments. So how did I help out the situation? First, I let him know I'm on his side and it wasn't a competition. Next, I showed and encouraged him to share in giving the hugs...randomly (you should have seen the shock on their faces...LOLOL). Additionally, I became more inclusive by inviting his thoughts and experiences to the conversation and it made a huge difference.

Mother's Day can start out being the pits: That's when you realize that you aren't the mother – but it gets better

I used to loathe Mother's Day when my daughter was young. It was always that subtle reminder that, although, I was the mother the other 364 days, I wasn't on this day. On this day, I felt as though I was just the lady who was married to the father. If anything special was done, it would have to end early so she could be picked up and taken to where her mother was supposed to be. Whether she was going to be with her mother or not, a point was made to remind me that Mother's Day wasn't mine. So this is what we did. We would go to the early worship service and have breakfast together afterwards. After breakfast, we would go home and I would pack her things so she could go see her mother. That went on for years—and then one day, she said she wasn't going and she wanted to stay home with me for Mother's Day! I was ecstatic. Honestly, I felt a little sadness for her mother; but it passed. As I stated before, my second husband's children were older when we became a family, so I had already worked through some things. I would always get a call or a text from each one letting me know I was loved, and how much they appreciated my role in their lives. And just like that, Mother's Day was no longer the pits.

Get ready for the return: When they come back from the other house, you may have to reprogram or deprogram

Here's where it gets sticky—and this is mostly when the blend is "home base" for the child; or simply put, your house is where they live full time. Yes, it's great when they go away for the weekend or the long holiday because you have time to yourself; however, if the homes and expectations are completely the opposite of yours, then get ready for the return. Prepare yourself for the "deprogramming/reprogramming" that will need to take place. Honestly, I don't think it matters as to the age of the child (I've had all ages). When they come back to you or come to you (if you're the "other home"), you'll have to redo everything that you've done. The reason is kids don't always adapt very well or very quickly to their surroundings. It's confusing for them to remember who does what at which house. Usually, all it takes is a simple, "Look at me—you're here now" (in a calm and loving voice) statement from mom and dad to bring them back to reality. I know it sounds simple—and yes, it's just that simple.

Now here's the reminder: THEY DIDN'T ASK FOR THIS SITUATION, SO BE PATIENT!!! Wow, that's my first "all caps" sentence 💻...That felt great! We tend to blame the children for the adult mistakes, and then get angry when they respond to the anger. The return is just as difficult for them as it is for you. The best way to address it is to let them tell you what they did on their own terms. If you ask too many questions, it's like you're fishing. If you don't ask any questions, then it seems like you don't care. Listen, you know your kids and you know their personality. If something seems unusual, then you push. If not, let them share as they wish. Again, this bit of advice is really more for the "home base" blend than for the "other home".

You didn't birth them and they didn't start with you: Once you realize this, your expectation of them becomes easier

This first came to me when I was serving as Youth Minister at my father's church. I often found myself having to calm youth workers down because they were angry at the kids and didn't understand what was wrong with them. The more I thought about it and the more I experienced it, I realized the problem wasn't the kids—it was us. We needed to realize these were not our children, and not only did we not raise them ourselves, but we were putting the expectations of our own children on the ones we were ministering to at the time. It's like this: You didn't birth the ones coming to you, and more than likely, you didn't raise them; so what you see, in essence is really what you get. If you want them to take on your values and your morals, then you will have to teach them your values and your morals. Notice I said "teach" and not "force". I've learned the best way to show children of any age something new is to do it in love and to teach by action. Live your values and your morals, and they will eventually pick it up. You'll find them curious and asking questions about your actions—and right there is your teaching moment. And a gentle reminder is this: If they don't, it's okay. You'll still be alright.

When your love is second: No matter what you do, you aren't number one in their lives

I once worked at a day care center as an assistant teacher. On one particular occasion, it was closing time and there was one little boy left. We called his mother over and over again; however, there was no answer. The little boy—realizing we were getting worried—reassured us his mother was coming. As the time got later, I was prepared to take him home with me and let her figure it out. Well, just as we were locking up, in walks his mother. She was so high she couldn't talk. I was so angry and was ready to give her the whole "I should call protective services on you" speech; but just as I was opening my mouth, the little boy squealed (yes, he squealed) in excitement and yelled, "I told you she was coming". I know you're wondering why I shared that story. I shared it because no matter what you do as the "other mother" or the "other father" at the very beginning, unless the circumstances are unique, you won't be number one. In fact, you may never be number one, but you will be in the number. As time passes, you may even alternate between number 1, 2, and maybe 3 and 4—depending on what's going on in their lives at the time. Honestly, to this day, I still struggle with that fact; however, each day, I remind myself if I stay in my lane and walk in my purpose for their lives, then that's what matters the most.

I'll take them with me: Again, knowing when the answer should be "No"

Earlier, I mentioned both parents must be involved when it comes to the blended family. It's easy, however, for one to take the more dominant role when it comes to activities and going places. My husband worked a lot and had crazy hours; so when he came home, it was nothing for me to take the kids and do something with them—even if it was gathering around the television to watch a show. I quickly found that once I started, not only was it always expected, but he was missing out on spending time with them. Not only that, but I started to feel taken advantage of which then led to feelings of resentment—neither one was good. Although I should have said something early on, I didn't and that I would change. It's one of those things that when I did push to have him participate with us, especially if we were all in the house, I wondered what took me so long. There's a movie that I like and in it, there is an ambitious older brother and the carefree younger brother. Towards the end of the movie, the younger brother tells the older brother that he never showed up because he knew the older brother would always be there to run the company. My husband never thought about having to take care of the kids because he knew I would always be there. He had no idea and I said nothing. Don't wait. Tell them now to join you and the kids.

Dad, where are you?: I can only do this if you help me

One of the most important things you can do to make this blend work is to let Dad know he's a part of the process. In all honesty, he's got to be involved; because not only do the kids need to see him, but they need to see him loving you. Here's the thing: You really don't know what they're being told when they aren't with you (I'm going to discuss this more later on), so since actions speak louder than words, what better way for them to form their own ideas and opinions by seeing him involved in the life of the blend? So, go ahead, tell him you need his help. I'll wait....now that wasn't hard was it?

What happens to them when we don't work out – What about the kids when we experience divorce and another family shattering?

I shared earlier what it was like blending #1 daughter with #2 husband. It wasn't easy, but it happened. The most important thing is communication. Remind the child often that your love won't stop and, if other children are introduced, our love for them won't decrease or end. Children need reassurance that the ones they trust the most will be there for them and still care. Here's the interesting thing that son from #2 husband recently brought up. He's almost 23, but he still wants to know that with all of the stuff he's done and all the bad decisions he's made, if anything were to happen to the family, he wants the assurance I will always be Ma Dana. Nothing is wrong and his dad and I are fine, but when he asked, I had to tell him he would always be my son. Crazy huh? My children never cease to amaze me.

Oh no, not again: And then there were 4 – having to start all over again and blend 4 families

So, when I remarried, I found myself having to re-blend because he had three children: two biological and one he inherited. In addition, I had my one, which meant there were four. Not too bad. Plus, this time around, I have some experience under my belt, so I better knew what to expect. My girl was the oldest (originally an only child) and being naturally bossy, I think she liked the fact of being the oldest and being able to tell the others what to do. I think they got along well. For the parents, it meant everybody knowing what was happening. So, I told husband #1 I was remarrying. Husband #2 told wife #1 he was remarrying. Husband #1 wanted to meet husband #2. Wife #1 wanted to meet wife #2. I know. That's a lot, but it was important that everyone involved was comfortable with the other. Remember I told you mothers want to know what's going on with their children? Well, so do fathers. They want to know the man who is involved in the life of their children. Now, here's the reality: We don't have to love each other, but we do have to respect each other. At some point, you have to trust the other to do the right thing. Remember, it's not about you, it's about the kids.

Roll your eyes at me one more time: Dealing with the ones who don't want to be a family

Each child has their own idea of family, and when the blended family is not their idea, you certainly know it. You deal with everything from a funky attitude, to poked out lips, to sucking of the teeth, to talking back. So how did I handle it? I told this particular daughter I was not going to tolerate it—and if she wanted to be with me, then this is what our family looked like: blended. That was one of the hardest things for me to do because I would do anything to keep her happy; but if I allowed the behavior to continue, it would have poisoned the family. And so, after a couple of weeks of, "No you can't come over", the message was received and the attitude adjustment took place and we all lived happily ever after. I'm just kidding, but we all did live.

I know you want her, but I'm the one here: What to do when they really do want their mother

So here's my experience with the first one that was the lesson for the rest: Mother wasn't around, but there was a semblance of a relationship. One day, she came home from a visit and cried. This wasn't normal, and she eventually verbalized she missed her mother. I didn't get emotional nor did I fly off the handle because of her statement. Instead, I held her in my lap (she was about 7 or 8); told her I understood and I loved on her like crazy. It wasn't necessary for me to say much; but I wanted to let her know her feelings were valid and although her mother wasn't there, I was. Please note: I didn't say much. Sometimes all they need is a listening ear and a loving hug.

No, I will not go for you, but I can meet you there: School issues with the kids

One of the early mistakes I made was volunteering to go to the school for a parent-teacher conference. I'm not even sure how it happened (probably one of those times I was trying to fix it 🖥); but all of a sudden, I found myself being called when they acted up in class—taking time off from work to do the "pop-up"—or running up when they forgot lunch. Yeah, that got old...but not until I stopped it. You'll have to realize it really does "take a village" and the chief is a part of the village. Communicate on a regular basis as to the responsibility of each and offer to go along. That way, the teacher knows that the kids have a true support system.

We're not made out of money: And don't just call when you need money

I guess this one is pretty straight-forward. As parents, so often we want to give our children everything. They don't have to work for anything, and as a result, you become the "cash cow". Let me tell you how it happened for us. For a very long time, I worked and made good money. During some budget cuts, I was laid off and that meant the household income was cut in half; and it also meant we had to budget carefully—not knowing how long it would take me to find another job. Now that I think about it, this may actually be when I learned to say no! We were always the ones who had the funds, but those funds were now needed to maintain our household. One day we woke up and realized the only time we heard from some of them was when they needed or wanted something. So here's my tip: WAKE UP!

I'm not the enemy: Establishing your role and destroying the "stepmother" stigma

It's all Cinderella's fault. That's where it all started: the wicked step-mother persona. In actuality, not all stepmothers are wicked and not all mothers are wonderful, but that's another book 💻. When I discovered my voice with the first child, I mentioned earlier the first thing that came out was, "If I was going to do anything to her, I would have already done it." In my family, there is no such thing as step-love, so there is no such thing as step-parent. It's amazing how that statement seemed to quiet all of the "noise" that was attempting to cause a divide in the relationship. Oh, don't get me wrong, I had to say it too many times to too many people, but it was the action that made the difference. Now here's the thing; I had to find a medium because I didn't want to set the example she could do what she wanted without me taking the role of disciplinarian—for fear of being considered the "wicked stepmother". What became more important to me was the relationship I had with the kids—and not the relationship I had with the outsiders looking in on us. In establishing the relationship, it's imperative to let them know that you are not the enemy—regardless of what they may have been told.

Dad, you tell Mama I'm here to help and not take over: Dad will need to do the introductions

The situation is already stressed; so another woman (me) entering the picture doesn't help at all. That's the reason it's important for Dad to make the introductions and possibly even establish clear roles. In my situation, for the most part, I had it easy. Sure, there were some stressful times—okay lots of stressful times—but because I refused to major in minor problems, the situations didn't get out of hand. Once all of us spoke and we understood the values, beliefs and morals for each family setting, the goal was the children's well-being. Now, I know people talk about co-parenting, but that didn't work for us. Simply put—co-parenting involves both parents working together to raise a child even though they are divorced, separated or no longer living together. It's a little more involved than shared custody because the two work closely together and communicate on a regular, sometimes, daily basis. Again, it didn't work in my situation; but I have family members who co-parent and its works beautifully for them. Do what works best for you.

No, we can't be besties: Setting boundaries with the other mother(s)

I like the mothers. I have even ministered to one of them on several occasions, but we're not best friends. We respect each other, we share information with each other, but I don't think we consider each other as friends. Even sitting here, I can't even see us as friends because we live different lives. We have different likes, and other than the kids, we really don't have much to talk about. How do I know? I know because her number is not the one I call when I need to talk. I don't feel bad about it nor do I feel guilty about it. Don't put yourself in a position where you feel obligated to have an amazing relationship with the other mother(s). If you're able to communicate, great! Now, if it happens that you become besties…wonderful!

It's okay to say no: You don't always have to say yes to make them like you

One of the hardest things, or rather, one of the major challenges I had when we blended, was telling the kids, "no". It was stressful for me because 1) I hate confrontation; and 2) I thought they would see me as the wicked stepmother; and 3) I didn't want that. Well, what I soon realized is if I was going to have the role of parent, then I needed to get over my "challenges" and deal with the task at hand. I learned how to say no to them without experiencing feelings of guilt or sadness. And believe it or not, it wasn't that difficult. Not only did they accept and respect me more, but they realized that I wasn't a pushover.

No matter how hard you try: Sometimes they just won't understand you

I've always said that, "Some people learn the easy way—some people learn the hard way, but no matter what, you will learn". Get this: No matter how hard you try, sometimes they just won't get it. You can show them, you can teach them, you can fuss, nag, and scream, but they won't get what you say; they won't get what you do, and they won't get you. But don't stop, because one day it will click, and you will be understood. Your hugs and kisses will make sense. Your worry will be understood and your long conversations will mean more than you can ever imagine.

No regrets: Even if it doesn't work out like you planned, rework the plan and count it as part of the journey

I shared earlier these tips are what worked for me. Needless to say, what I have presented to you is not the draft, but the final product. Learning all of this took time, effort, tears, prayers (lots of prayers), sweat, frustration, aggravation, giving up, giving in, throwing in the towel, and more. However, take what you can use, tweak them to your situation and be patient. It's not going to happen overnight and some things may even change in the middle—so, remain flexible and learn from the stumbling blocks as they became your stepping stones.

We come as a package deal: Be careful as these words may backfire

Sometimes taking a stand and giving an ultimatum doesn't work out in our advantage. For example, declaring that you and the kids are a package deal forces the other to choose between the package deal or the single deal waiting on the side without the drama. Now don't get me wrong, yes, you must protect, stand up for, and think about the kids; however, I think in this case, it's not what you say, but how you say it. Letting someone know you love your kids should be presented in such a way that you don't look like the bully on the playground threatening to leave and take your ball or jump rope with you. This is also a case where actions speak louder than words because, honestly, if you've dated for quite some time, they already know the relationship you and your children have by what they see. Therefore, there is no need to say anything. And, for real, if you have to make the claim, then you already know it's not a good thing.

Vacation and other times when our plans don't line up

I spoke briefly about holidays and school breaks earlier, but I wanted to deal with another issue and that is, what to do when our plans don't line up with one another. Earlier in the tips, I shared a story with you about my experience when I was forced to explain. This is the full story of the account. When #2 son came to live with us, he visited his mom on the weekends. It seemed everything was going well until we decided to move! Yes, we moved from one county to another; and you would have thought that it was World War 3 going on! The problem is we did not check/clear it with his mother before telling him and to be candid, not only were we still in the early stages, it never crossed our minds to do so because after all, he was living with us and we were responsible for him. Receiving the call actually floored me because I had never been spoken to in that manner before by an "adult." And again, he was living with us and we were taking care of him. The call came while my husband and I were in the car on the way home. She was screaming so loud that my husband heard. He sort of chuckled in an, "I was waiting for her to call" sort of way. I told her we would call her back when we got in the house. When I hung up, I think the look on my face let him know what I was thinking. Needless to say, when we arrived at home, I handed him the phone and he called. While I won't give details, I will say this: our moving plans remained the same. Tip to remember? Like the song says, "You gotta know when to hold 'em, know when to fold 'em". Choose your battles wisely and do what you can to work it out. Negotiation and compromise are great tools to have—and using them is NOT a sign of weakness, but a sign of wisdom!

Dealing with the family budget

It has been shown that many marriages end due to either infidelity or finances. Those two coupled with trying to raise a blended family on a budget can sometimes take its toll. Think about it. You're married and used to a certain financial flow in the household, and then here comes more people cutting into the budget. There are people that you really are not responsible to support; but nevertheless, they need braces or new shoes or school fees—and the money has to come from somewhere! So what did we do? We helped out when and where we could and learned to say, "No". That wasn't an easy thing for either of us because we wanted to provide, but we had to be realistic in that we would be in a difficult situation if we gave what we had. As the kids got older and got jobs, we didn't mind helping out when we saw them putting forth an effort. The example I'll use is a recent trip to St. Croix. We invited the youngest daughter to go with us and told her in enough time that she would be responsible for her own plane ticket and a portion of her housing cost. She worked and saved to pay for both and even had some left over for spending money. That experience taught her to be financially responsible and that travel is a possibility in her life. As the adage says, "Give them a hand up not a handout".

Not all of them stay

I was blessed in that the ones I inherited wanted to be a part of the family in the beginning. And then something happened. I really don't know what. The oldest boy chose not to come and not to hang out with us. We didn't force it. We didn't ask a lot of questions, but we think he had a hard time fitting in. There came a point in his life he wanted to do his own thing; and what he wanted to do wasn't what we did. So we had to let him go on his journey. We still count him as one of the four. He has a family of his own and he calls every now and again to speak to his dad about life and that's a good thing.

No blame game

Now my friend, this is a tough one for me, and let me tell you why. In all of the tips, I know it seems like life was perfect, but guess what? That's not the case. It's not always going to be perfect and it's not always going to go the way you want. I inherited four beautiful children, and of the four, one left, one lived with us briefly, one still lives with us and one is currently incarcerated. When he was arrested, one of the things we could not and would not do was blame each other. Our son made bad decisions and has to pay for them. But in the meantime, he still calls and we talk about everything under the sun. We write and send pictures to keep him connected; we send money every now and again for commissary; and, when we're able, we visit. He's still ours and we'll always love him…without blame.

Breathe....

Go somewhere and sit down – Take a time-out for yourself

Believe it or not, I would sometimes find myself putting myself in time-out. It wasn't them, it was me. And when it was me, I didn't want to attack them. So, I would go somewhere and sit down and breathe. You see, sometimes, this blended family journey can knock the wind right out of your sail—and all you want to do is go somewhere and sit down. It's alright. It's for the best. Trust me; for the sake of all involved....do it.

Look forward to the "away" weekends: Celebrate you when they go for the weekend visit

I must be honest—not that I haven't already been honest—but here I'm going to be REAL honest. I would look forward to those away weekends! That was my time for me. I would get my hair done or get my nails done or nothing at all. It meant I didn't have to get up on a Saturday morning and fix breakfast or take anybody anywhere. I learned to use that time to celebrate me in all my "me-ness" and without the feeling of guilt. Enjoy the time. Stop worrying about what they're doing and who he has around them and celebrate the moment. Life becomes much more tolerable when you're not stressed out and fixated on what goes on at his house. As long as they are safe...then all is well. Celebrate!

Sometimes you just have to be quiet and stay out of it – There are some times you need to let them handle it and work it out

One of the lessons I've learned is to know when to stay out of a conversation I wasn't invited to join. Sometimes, as difficult as it may be, I have to stay quiet and not put in my two cents. Not easy!!! I'm a fixer and a caretaker, so I often find myself trying to fix a person, a situation, an argument...whatever...it's just what I do! You may find yourself in the same situation, so here's my tip: Be quiet and let them handle it or let it fix itself. You can't fix everybody.

Not perfect but peaceful – This process isn't perfect, but you will have peace... moments of peace

I chose this topic because it's important to understand this blend is not going to be perfect. One of the goals is to get everyone to live together in peace. Honestly, I did it so we wouldn't kill each other. Now, here's the thing. The peace I needed most came when child #1 met husband #2 (not her father). What an explosion! Again, I had to understand the "why" of her actions and not the "what" (you'll see this a lot). For most of her life, it was the three of us, and after her dad and I divorced, here comes a stranger into her life saying he loved her mother. For her, she needed to "flex" and let him know she was in charge and was assigned to protect me (or so she thought). I had to let her know I didn't want to choose and it wasn't necessary to do so. I had to explain she was and would always be my baby and his children would become her brothers and sisters. I had to explain to her my love for her would NEVER change. And then I had to step back and let their relationship happen. It wasn't perfect, but it was peaceful because they figured it out. See, after I did all I could to set the atmosphere for peace, I had to step back and let it happen—intervening when needed in order to keep the peace. Although her "what" of her action was attitude and much mouth; the "why" was simply fear she was losing me. When that was addressed, the peaceful moments became more and more frequent. And today, after 12 years, they are best of buds. Peace at last!

New memories together – Making new memories as a family without ignoring what already is

One of the things I loved to do was take the kids to a park and take pictures. We'd print them out, frame them, and hang them on the walls. It made our home look like our home. There were some pictures that they took before they even knew me and I let them hang those… in their room. We have to remember before you, they were. They were with someone else and they lived a life with someone else. No matter what you do, those are still their memories and must be acknowledged as such, and the same goes for traditions. Learn to incorporate their memories and traditions with your memories and traditions to create new memories and traditions together. If they don't have any, then there's no excuse. Be creative. Get excited. And watch the bond get stronger.

Truth is – remembering why you're doing this

Sometimes, in my time out period, I would re-evaluate why I was doing this. Why was I raising other people's kids like my own? Why should I care? I can be married to him and not deal with them. I can distance myself and let him handle his and I handle mine. I married him, not them. And then, I glance at those pictures on the wall; or I look at a text message I got for Mother's Day and I remember Daddy's words: "There's no such thing as step-love." And I realize I love these kids—all of them like they were my own. I love them because they are a part of him. I love them because they made my world amazing. I love them so much that I wish I had them myself. And it's all good...until the next time.

EPILOGUE

Well, that's it. I've shared my experiences with you on how I made our blended family work. What started out as 35 tips soon became 40 and then 51. I'm not sure if I have more, but if I do, you'll be the first to know about it when you see Volume 2. In the meantime, take this guide, read it, share it, and then apply it to your own life situation. Remember that no situation is the same and you will more than likely need to tweak them to fit your life.

If you have any questions, please feel free to email me at <u>revdana.</u> <u>ashton@gmail.com</u>. Make sure you put "YMO Question" in the subject line so that I'll know it's you and I'll respond as quickly as possible. I'm also available to speak at your conferences, retreats, workshops, or other events. In addition, you can send the request to my assistant, Josephine Gupton at <u>edwardsjosephine22@yahoo.com</u> and she'll send you the speaking contract. I'm also in the process of putting the tips on audio so you can listen to them during your commute or your work-out time. That's really going to be fun.

I'm praying and cheering for you so join me as I celebrate you and your blended family!

 Rev. Dana Porter Ashton is the youngest of four daughters of the late Rev. Dr. William Robert and Mrs. Doris Ann Porter. She attended public schools in Washington, D.C., then continued her education at Howard University, where she graduated with a Bachelor's Degree in Human Development. Rev. Dana completed her Master's Degree in Christian Counseling from Maple Springs Baptist Bible College and Seminary, and earned her Master of Divinity Degree from Howard University.

Rev. Dana is an ordained Itinerant Elder in the African Methodist Episcopal Church and is currently the proud Pastor of Union Chapel AME Church, Cambridge, MD. She also serves as an instructor for the Baltimore Annual Conference Board of Examiners, the educational body that prepares ministers for Ordination in the AME Church and as the Worship Leader for the Second Episcopal District Women In Ministry. Rev. Dana has traveled extensively throughout the country and abroad preaching and teaching the gospel of Jesus Christ, and directing and singing with many choirs. She has coordinated and spoken at various retreats, workshops, and programs. Rev. Dana served under her father for several years and has a powerfully uncanny love for those who have given up and have no hope.

Prior to her pastoral appointment, Rev. Dana served as pastor of Bethel AME Church, Chesapeake City, and as the assistant to Dr. Frank Madison Reid, III, at Bethel AME Church in Baltimore, Maryland. God has anointed her with a compassionate heart and healing power, which led her to develop the Healing Hearts Women's Fellowship, where she ministered to women who have been hurt in any manner.

Rev. Dana is the wife of her high school sweetheart, Maurice Anthony Ashton. She is the mother of Brittany Alexandria, her joy,

Godmommy to Kisha, her heart, Ma Dana to Marcellus, Malcolm, and Monay, her angels, and Nana to Dionte, Zion, Elijah, and Dayna Amaya, her precious ones.

Her favorite scripture is John 15:16 which confirmed that God had an assignment specifically for her and her favorite word that God uses is "**BEHOLD**", which reminds her that God is always up to something.